MW01257530

This Notebook Belongs To

____

Made in the USA
Las Vegas, NV
24 February 2024

86252306R00057